The Herbal Project Book

Joanna Sheen

PHOTOGRAPHY BY JACQUI HURST

MEREHURST

Published in 1995 by Merehurst Limited,
Ferry House, 51–57 Lacy Road, Putney, London SW15 1PR

ISBN 1 85391 342 1

A catalogue record of this book is available from the British Library.

Edited by **Heather Dewhurst**
Designed by **Lisa Tai**
Styling by **Jacqui Hurst**

Typeset by Servis Filmsetting Ltd., Manchester
Colour separation by Global Colour, Malaysia
Printed in Singapore by Craftprint

Contents

❧

Introduction

Herbs have played an important part in the everyday life of mankind for centuries – they can decorate, heal, soothe, and enhance the flavour of food, which has to make them one of the most valuable groups of plants that you could grow in your garden. If you are short of garden space many herbs can now be purchased fresh or still growing from supermarkets and delicatessens.

The beautiful soft greys and blues associated with herbs make them a joy to look at in the garden and a useful palette of colours to mix with other flowers and plants in decorations and arrangements. Herbs should never be considered too humble to play a part in celebrations and special occasions. The magic power of herbs has given them a position of respect throughout history and they were always part of any important occasion. Whether you use herbs in a small way, such as including some rosemary in a bridal bouquet, or give them a larger role, such as decorating tables with mixed herb arrangements, herbs always look attractive.

Growing & drying herbs

In the Middle Ages, the mistress of the manor house had her own still room – a place where she concocted her household recipes and remedies using herbs. She would have made pot pourris, healing balms and potions to perfume and disinfect. Unfortunately, these household crafts have long since been superseded by aerosols and much more potent medicine, and herbs have been relegated to the kitchen. However, using herbs need not be limited to flavouring food. Try incorporating them in your flower arrangements and once you start you will be hooked – they seem to add a much more subtle dimension and interest compared with popular garden foliage.

Many herbal plants are fairly small in scale and, as such, do not mix with larger garden plants such as gladioli or enormous chrysanthemums. However, used in reasonable bunches, as opposed to individual stems, they make a good contribution to small and medium-sized arrangements and add a lovely country simplicity as well as a traditional touch to your decorating. Country-style arrangements and traditional displays with flowers in dainty Victorian-style containers and baskets all cry out for herbs to be included. Try incorporating them into your more usual choice of greenery and you will be pleased with the extra detail and perfume they bring to a flower display.

GROWING HERBS
You will find that herbs are a very simple group of plants to grow in the garden. Start by growing a collection of half a dozen that appeal to you the most and see how you get on. I would recommend growing one of the mints but beware how fast they spread – they will soon take over a large area. The best way to combat this is to plant the mint in a large sheet of plastic to inhibit the amount of space it can take up.

Thyme and sage are also relatively easy to grow, and growing a bay hedge can be very useful. The bay leaves can be used in cooking but are also a very good basic foliage for many arrangements, both herbal and non-herbal. Fennel is another herb that is very straightforward to grow; the flowers can be used fresh or dried in arrangements and the leaves are useful in many cookery recipes. You could also try growing basil and parsley, although these may be more difficult. Basil seems to perform well for some and not for others, and likewise parsley. But have a go and you could be one of the lucky ones!

If you do not have room in a flowerbed outside, try growing some herbs in pots on a balcony or even indoors. I find that outdoor herbs are always the most healthy – those grown indoors can be subjected to too much heat or light and become pale and leggy.

DRYING HERBS
Herbs can all be air dried by hanging them in small bunches, tied with elastic bands, in a warm airy place. However, if you want a small amount of herbs for culinary use or for use in pot pourri, you can also dry them in a microwave. Use a couple of sheets of kitchen paper as a base and lay the herbs in small pieces on the paper. Place in the microwave and cook on a medium to high setting for a couple of minutes and then check to see whether they are sufficiently dry. This method

does not work for herbs you want to see in an arrangement as the drying process can make the herbs very brittle and they can only be dried in small pieces, but it can be very handy.

DISPLAYING HERBS

Air dried bunches of herbs look very attractive hung in rows across a kitchen ceiling. Alternatively you can arrange bunches of herbs along the top of tall kitchen cupboards to achieve a similar effect. An old laundry airer suspended from the ceiling is another very effective way of displaying your harvest!

Herbs are such informal plants that dried bunches can look terrific tied with a simple ribbon or thick string and laid in fireside baskets or tra-ditional garden trugs. Their soft colours blend well with many other dried ingredients. They look very pretty included in a romantic garland of flowers for a country style bedroom decoration.

Dried herbs are also invaluable for scented pillows and sachets. Hops are well known for their sleep-inducing properties but many pleasant blends of herbs can relax you and help you sleep just by giving out such a wonderful perfume. Add a soft scent to your linens and airing cupboard by tying bunches of herbs with ribbons and suspending them from shelves or hooks in the cupboard.

Add either fresh or dried herbs to your flower arrangements for a lovely country simplicity.

Basket of herbs

This rustic trug of herbs and daisies will last well as the flowers are in plenty of water and the herbs in pots. It would make a lovely display for a kitchen windowsill or table, and the herbs can then be used for cooking when needed.

Basket of herbs

This is a very informal basket arrangement that would look charming on a kitchen table and can come in very useful when you need a sprig of basil or parsley. Herbs do not stay fresh in an arrangement for long, so this is the perfect answer – potted herbs together with flowers in separate containers of water. For this arrangement you will need a selection of abundant potted herbs – I have used 4 pots of basil, 3 pots of parsley, 2 pots of purple sage and some small white daisies.

INGREDIENTS

Herbs and flowers, see above

A rustic trug, approximately 35cm (14in) long

2 jam jars

Cut-flower food, optional

ə

1 Make sure the pots of basil have been well watered and place them in position in the trug or basket. Never use weak or weedy specimens as they will spoil the overall effect.

2 Fill the jam jars with water and, if you wish, some cut-flower food. Place some sprays of small white daisies in the jars at varying heights. Add the daisies to the basket.

Many other flowers would be suitable if you do not have daisies.

3 Place the pots of parsley and sage in position to fill the basket. Try to choose herbs that contrast in colour as well as in leaf shape and texture, to give the best combination.

Kitchen wreath & Herbal horseshoe

This wreath is perfect for the kitchen with the amusing addition of wine corks and pots of beans. The horseshoe would make an unusual good luck token for a bride – it's fairly heavy but it looks lovely!

Kitchen wreath

With kitchen space often at a premium, this herbal decoration is ideal for hanging on the wall or cupboard door where it won't take up any worktop space. The bay leaves can be used fresh and allowed to dry in position, or used once they have dried out. You will also need some wheat, box leaves, marjoram, sage and a large hydrangea head. Finally, you will need to drink a few bottles of wine to collect the corks necessary for the decoration, but that may not be too great a hardship!

INGREDIENTS

Herbs and flowers, see above

Glue gun and glue

A twiggy ring, 20cm (8in) in diameter

6 miniature flowerpots

Kidney beans, mung beans and haricot beans

❧

1 Glue the bay leaves either individually or in sprays onto the wreath base, making a curve that covers about two-thirds of the ring. Cut the ears of wheat so their stems are very short and place a small group on each side of the wreath on the bay leaves. Glue in position.

2 Place the corks in the middle of the decorated curve, gluing them on individually. Add some sprays of box on either side of the corks. Then add some small sprays of dried grey sage and bunches of marjoram, leaving some gaps for the terracotta flowerpots to fill.

3 Once you feel the wreath is full enough, add the little flowerpots, three on each side of the corks. Glue the dried beans into the pots. If you have not got these particular pulses, then lentils, pasta, other varieties of dried herbs or small pieces of dried fruit would work as alternatives.

Herbal horseshoe

A horseshoe is meant to bring good luck and makes a lovely wedding gift or good luck token. This horseshoe is one from a local horse but if you have trouble finding real horseshoes try asking a local riding stables or blacksmith and they may be able to help you. The shoe will need cleaning before you use it – plenty of sandpaper and elbow grease to remove any rust, and metal cleaner to bring out the shine. Then give the horseshoe a coat of varnish to prevent any further rusting. For the decoration you will need bay leaves, some sprays of box leaves and 7 or 8 small pink roses.

INGREDIENTS

Raffia

Horseshoe

Glue gun and glue

Flowers and foliage, see above

Cinnamon sticks

Silver rose wire

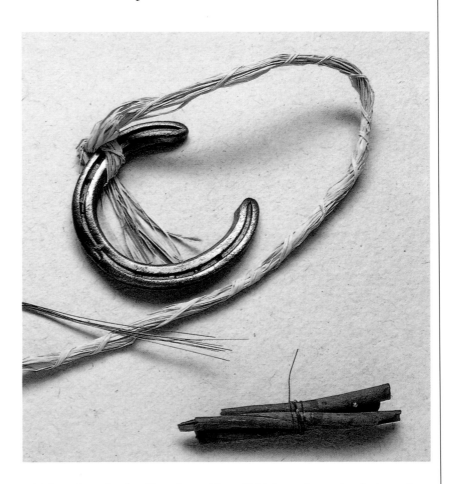

1 Take a length of raffia, about 60cm (2ft) long, from the skein and twist it until it resembles a thick cord. If it is a little unmanageable, twist a separate strand of raffia around it to hold it together. Knot the raffia around both ends of the horseshoe and glue it at the back to ensure that it stays in position. Glue a small raffia bow to the centre of the twisted raffia strand for added decoration.

2 *Glue some sprays of bay on either side of the centre of the shoe and add some small sprays of box. Other green herbs or foliage could be used if you cannot find either of these varieties. Make a small bundle of cinnamon sticks by wrapping wire around them.*

3 *Wrap raffia around the cinnamon bundle to conceal the wire, and glue it to the centre of the horseshoe. Finally glue in the roses on either side of the cinnamon.*

Bathroom swag

*The perfect answer to bathroom decoration, this swag
can be hung in the bathroom either horizontally or
vertically and will take up no surface or floor space at all!
The glass nuggets catch the light and add a pretty sparkle
to the arrangement.*

$\mathcal{B}$athroom swag

Bathrooms are always difficult rooms to furnish as there is usually little or no spare space. This wall-hanging swag is a delightful alternative to having a flower arrangement in the bathroom and is moderately quick to make up. The glass nuggets arranged decoratively in the shells are readily available from many garden centres, florists and craft stores – they are intended for flower arrangement but have many other uses! You will also need a bunch each of dried green honesty, dried or preserved box, bay, hydrangea, marjoram and wheat, 3 bell cups and 4 heads of peony.

INGREDIENTS

Flowers and foliage, see above

Glue gun and glue

Piece of hardboard, approximately 45 × 15cm (18in × 6in), with 'D' ring hanger

Half a jar of green glass nuggets

4 large shells

Liquorice stems

Raffia

🌰

1 Take small sprays of honesty and bay and glue them to the outside of the hardboard. Add some sprigs of box to make an even frill all the way around the board, leaving the centre bare. Glue the glass nuggets individually into the shells, and place the shells randomly on the display.

2 Glue the shells firmly in position, then add the bell cups and peony heads. Add some bundles of wheat ears to the outer edge of the arrangement and some small bunches of marjoram. Wrap the bundles of liquorice stems (or other twigs) with raffia and add them into the arrangement.

3 Fill any gaps in the arrangement with hydrangea pieces and extra bay or wheat. There are many possible variations. If you want to change the colour of the arrangement, substitute different coloured nuggets and other herbs and flowers.

$\mathcal{T}$eacup of herbs

This lovely arrangement of fresh herbs and pansies can be made in a very short time, entirely from your garden. The finished project is quite charming and would delight anyone as a gift or as a decoration for a summer tea table. You will need a mixed selection of herbs, such as rosemary, rue (Jackman's Blue), grey sage and some small violas or a selection of pansies.

INGREDIENTS

Scissors

Small piece of green florist's foam

A cup and saucer

Flowers and herbs, see above

Fine rose wire, optional

Narrow purple ribbon, approximately 30cm (12in) long

1 Cut the foam so that it is fractionally larger than the diameter of the cup and press it in firmly. Soak the foam with water. Insert a selection of herbs into the foam all around the cup, making sure that you cover the foam completely.

2 Carefully add the violas to the arrangement. Their stalks are very soft so they do tend to break easily; if you find it impossible to push the stalks into the foam, gently wrap some fine rose wire around the stems to strengthen them. To complete the display, make a tiny bunch of the herbs and flowers used in the teacup, and tie it with the purple ribbon. This posy could then be laid on a matching saucer.

Topiary trees & Herbs in terracotta

These herbal topiary trees would make a lovely decoration for any room. The fresh herbs in terracotta are brightened by the addition of chilli peppers and kumquats.

Topiary trees

These tiny topiary trees are really gorgeous and will make a very attractive centrepiece or windowsill decoration. Although they look impressive, they are relatively easy to make. Most herbs can be used but avoid the softer herbs such as basil that might not last so well. To make a topiary tree, you will need a large bunch of thyme and a cinnamon stick for each tree, plus the herb of your choice. Here I used curry plant foliage for the medium-sized tree and golden sage for the largest tree.

INGREDIENTS

A small terracotta container

2 pieces of green florist's foam

Cinnamon stick, approximately 15cm (6in) long

Knife

Herb of your choice

Ribbon or small flowers for decoration, optional

≈

1 Fill the terracotta container with foam and soak well; cover any holes in the bottom of the container. Push the cinnamon stick into the foam and place the second piece of foam onto the stick. Cut the corners off this piece of foam to produce a spherical shape.

2 *Cover the base with a selection of greenery or the single herb used for the ball of the tree. Place pieces of herb at each side and at the top of the foam ball to give you the outer points of your circular shape.*

3 *Fill in the rest of the ball with small pieces of thyme, either placed singly or in small groups. Keep turning the tree as you are filling in the gaps so that the overall shape is as round as possible. Once the tree is complete, you could add further decoration, such as a ribbon or small flowerheads.*

Herbs in terracotta

Herbs make a delightful subject for an informal kitchen arrangement. Here herbs and some vegetables and fruit have been combined for an unusual combination. Any small vegetables could be substituted. The foliage and herbs can come from your garden or from a selection at the supermarket and florist's. You will need 7 or 8 pieces of bay, 7 large ivy leaves, and a bunch of rue (Jackman's Blue).

INGREDIENTS

Terracotta pot

Piece of green florist's foam

Small bundle of 0·71mm (22 gauge) florist's wires

1 Romanesco cauliflower

10 or more asparagus tips

7 kumquats

❧

1 Fill the terracotta pot with foam and soak well. Add the bay sprigs around the pot so that they almost cover the foam. Other medium-leaved greenery could be used instead, such as scented geranium leaves.

2 *Add the ivy leaves to the pot. If they have strong stems you can place them straight into the foam; if the stems are too flexible to do this, strengthen them with some wire wrapped around the stem. The foam should be completely covered by now.*

3 *Add the rue throughout the arrangement. Then wire the pieces of cauliflower by pushing a wire halfway through the stalk and twisting the two ends together to make a wire stem. Wire the asparagus and kumquats in the same way. Place these ingredients into the arrangement to complete the design.*

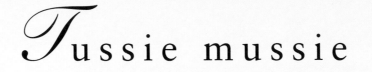

Tussie mussie

*This beautiful, fragrant posy has a hidden message
contained in the language of flowers, a popular Victorian
amusement. Whether or not you use flowers and herbs with a
hidden meaning, a tussie mussie would make a lovely gift.*

Tussie mussie

A tussie mussie is an old-fashioned posy that includes scented flowers to combat unpleasant smells in the vicinity, and in this case all the ingredients also carry a secret message using the language of flowers. Parsley means festivity, roses are for love, sage conveys esteem and ivy stands for friendship and fidelity – a lovely message to give a friend when visiting for a meal or for the weekend. You will need about 20 or 30 stems of parsley, 6 roses, 7–10 ivy leaves, depending on size, and a bunch of sage.

INGREDIENTS

Glue gun and glue

A lace frill to edge the posy

A foam posy holder (available from florists or garden centres)

Herbs and flowers, see above

A reel of silver rose wire

Ribbons, optional

ॐ

1 Glue the frill to the posy holder and place the ivy leaves in the foam around the edge of the bouquet. Put a rose in the centre and space the other five evenly around, leaving space for the other ingredients between them.

2 *Bunch the parsley three or more stems at a time, depending on how bushy it is, and wrap some fine wire around the stem to hold the bunch together. Place several bunches in the posy between the other ingredients so that the foam is well covered.*

3 *Take small pieces of sage, removing any leaves that are too long and would stick out too far, and place them into the bouquet. Sage has a fairly* woody stem and pushes into the foam easily so it does not need wiring. Make sure the foam is completely covered and then spray the posy with *water to help it remain fresh. Finally, tie a ribbon around the posy if you would like some extra decoration.*

Bath sachets & Pot pourri

Bath sachets filled with herbs from the garden will give you a soothing, relaxing bath. The herbal pot pourri is also made with garden produce and is much prettier than commercial varieties.

$\mathcal{B}$ath sachets

Using bath sachets is a lovely old-fashioned way of scenting your bath water, and makes a lovely change from bright pink bubble bath! You can use any number of herbal mixtures inside the bag – lavender is always successful as is fresh or dried rosemary. Dried roses or rosebuds are also a useful standby. If you want to strengthen the scent and the relaxing effect of the herbal bath, add a few drops of the matching essential oil to the water.

INGREDIENTS

Scissors

Calico or muslin

Herbs of your choice

Small elastic bands

Ribbon or cord

❧

1 *Cut out some squares of calico – about 22·5cm (9in) wide seems to be a workable size. If the pieces are cut any smaller you will not be able to fit the herbs inside. As an alternative to calico you could use muslin or any other inexpensive thin fabric.*

2 Lay a few sprigs of your chosen herbs in the centre of the square of fabric, gather up the sides and secure with an elastic band. It is just as easy to make several bags at a time as they can sit in a basket or bowl by the bath until they are needed.

3 Cut some long pieces of ribbon and tie them around each elastic band, adding a small bow if required. The ends of the ribbon can then be tied around the bath taps so that the bag dangles in the water. When the taps are turned on to fill the bath, the stream of water will pass through the sachet and perfume your bath.

$\mathscr{P}$ot pourri

Making your own pot pourri is always fun and herbs make very good pot pourri components. You can dry the herbs by placing them on a paper towel and cooking them in the microwave on medium to full power for 2 minutes. The perfume can be added with an essential oil so any herbal foliage can be used as the leaf base of this mixture. Here I used one cup of each of the following: rue leaves, angelica leaves, lemon balm, dark pink, scented rose petals, mixed pieces of spice – cloves, cinnamon and nutmeg, and lavender flowers. In addition you need 15g (½oz) orris root, 1 tsp any herbal essential oil or perfume oil (I used a mixture of marjoram and lavender) and a few small sprays of lavender to decorate.

INGREDIENTS

Pot pourri ingredients, see above

Bowl

Metal spoon

Large plastic bag

Elastic band

Container for pot pourri

Shells

Glue

ðŧ

1 Dry all the necessary ingredients and mix together in a bowl with the orris root and oil. Stir well, using a metal spoon (a wooden spoon would absorb the oil).

2 Tip the mixture into a large plastic bag and secure the top with an elastic band. Shake well and leave for a week or so to mature. The perfumes will blend together and smell far better if you are patient!

3 While the pot pourri is maturing, decorate a plain container in which you can display your pot pourri. Choose a container with a smooth surface (old Camembert cheese boxes work well), and glue on shells in a random design to cover it completely. Alternatively, you could decorate the box with spices or dried seedheads.

Celebration basket

This very special basket would make a wonderful centrepiece for a special occasion. Once made, it is very heavy and should be moved as little as possible.

Celebration basket

This magnificent arrangement is for a very special occasion and could be placed on the floor, on a side table or on the edge of a platform. Although this is a very large arrangement, items like bunches of grapes and artichokes can take up large amounts of the space and therefore save money on the flower content of the basket. To make this celebration basket you will need 2 bunches (10 stems) of stargazer lilies, a bunch of white spray carnations, 2 bunches of striped carnations, a bunch of white alstroemeria and 30 assorted stems of herbal and other greenery, including trails of ivy.

INGREDIENTS

Large, shallow basket, approximately 45cm (18in) long

Polythene

4 blocks of green florist's foam

Florist's tape

Foliage and flowers, see above

1 large bunch of purple grapes, 3 limes, 3 plums, 3 green apples, 3 globe artichoke heads, 3 purple and green kohlrabi or small purple-tinged turnips

Pointed wooden sticks, approximately 30cm (12in) long

❧

1 Line the basket carefully with polythene and place the four well-soaked blocks of foam into position. Tape them firmly to the polythene so that they do not move about. Place the stems of assorted greenery in position, ensuring there are long flowing pieces of ivy on each side of the basket and a good mass of green foliage covering the foam. Keep the foliage reasonably low and well below the handle of the basket.

2 Add the lilies, with one in the centre to give height and one trailing on each side to blend with the ivy. Remember that the lilies will be tightly shut when you arrange them and they will only open a day or so later, so leave room for them to expand! Add the other flowers in groups, leaving room at the front for the grapes and a space at the side for the other fruit.

3 Impale each vegetable and each piece of fruit, except the grapes, on a stick. Arrange the fruit in the foam in groups. The grapes can either have a substantial wire wrapped around the stem and then planted in the foam, or the bunch can just be laid in the arrangement. It is important to water the foam regularly as there will be many stems needing to take up water if the flowers are to survive for a reasonable length of time.

Kitchen
arrangement

*A bread board makes an ideal base for a
kitchen display – it can be hung on a wall, or
simply placed on a table. The bread rolls add an
interesting touch to the overall arrangement.*

Kitchen arrangement

This decorated bread board hangs on my wooden cooker hood and has looked very attractive for many years. It is important to give the finished arrangement a good coat of varnish to help it survive the grease and dust in the kitchen. The varnish makes it much easier to keep clean. The bread rolls should be dried in a slow oven and then heavily varnished. You will need some marjoram, bay leaves and wheat.

INGREDIENTS

Silver rose wire

Herbs and foliage, see above

A bread board, approximately 25cm (10in) in diameter, with 'D' ring hanger

6 cinnamon sticks

Glue gun and glue

4 assorted bread rolls

2 terracotta ornaments or flowerpots

6 slices each of dried orange and dried green grapefruit

Wood spray varnish

❧

1 Wire the ears of wheat into small clumps of three ears. Lay them onto the board and move them around until you are happy with their places. Then place the cinnamon sticks in position so that they cover the wheat stems. Glue them down firmly.

2 Glue in the bread rolls and terracotta ornaments. If you cannot find similar little jugs, terracotta pots would look fine. Glue in the marjoram to fill any gaps.

3 Add the fruit slices, if necessary cutting them in half so that they do not protrude too far. Then fill in any gaps with bay leaves. Finally, give the arrangement a good spray of wood varnish – outside, because of the fumes.

*S*uppliers

For details of dried flowers, craft ingredients, and pressed flower ingredients and oils by mail order; also two-day craft courses on flowers and other crafts:

Joanna Sheen Limited
PO Box 52
Newton Abbot
Devon TQ12 4QH

For pot pourri ingredients and oils, and details of shops throughout the country:

Culpeper Limited
21 Bruton Street
London W1X 7DA

For details of dried flowers by mail order and farm shop:

Caroline Alexander
The Hop Shop
Castle Farm
Shoreham
Sevenoaks
Kent TN14 7UB

ACKNOWLEDGEMENTS

Jacqui Hurst and Merehurst would like to thank the following for lending props for the photographs in this book: David Robertson and Peta Weston for creating the special backgrounds; and Margaret Check, Hazel Hurst and Nesta MacDonald who kindly lent their lace, table linen and crockery.